MW00897206

DIZZY DEAN

AND THE GASHOUSE GANG

Written by Carolyn E. Mueller
Illustrated by Ed Koehler

The name is J. Roy Stockton.

I'm a reporter and the St. Louis Cardinals
are my beat.

I'm here to tell you about a bunch of ballplayers
who look rough and play rougher.

We call 'em the "Gashouse Gang."

The leader of this gang is a few cards short of a full deck.

He changes his name as often as I change my underwear.

But that crazy pitcher has a knack for making batters look dizzy!

He claims a lot of different names. But we call him Dizzy. Dizzy Dean.

Off the field he's known to make trouble, especially with third baseman Pepper Martin.

One time, Cards manager Frankie Frisch was minding his own business when . . .

BAM!

A water balloon exploded right at his feet!

It's no better on the field. When Frank tells Dizzy to throw fastballs, Diz throws curves. When he says give 'em the curve, Diz brings the heat.

Dizzy and Pepper usually ham it up.

One hot summer day at the ballpark those two chowderheads decided to build a campfire . . .
RIGHT THERE ON THE FIELD!

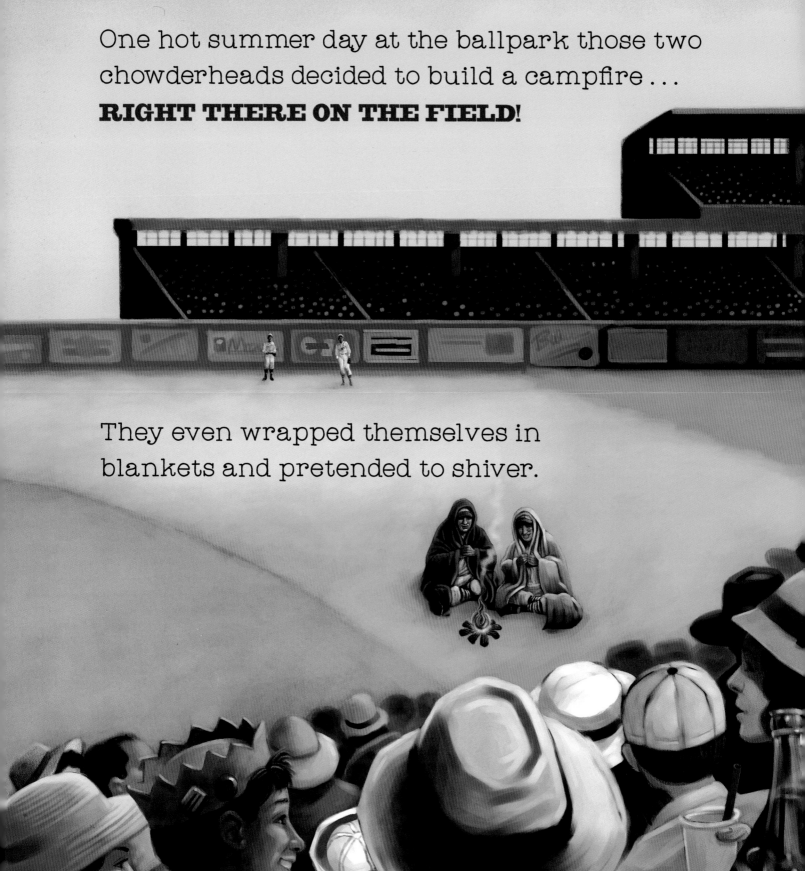

They even wrapped themselves in blankets and pretended to shiver.

The shenanigans didn't stop there.

Pepper once saw a hillbilly band outside the ballpark and snuck them into the clubhouse!

Poor Frank had a regular hootenanny on his hands.

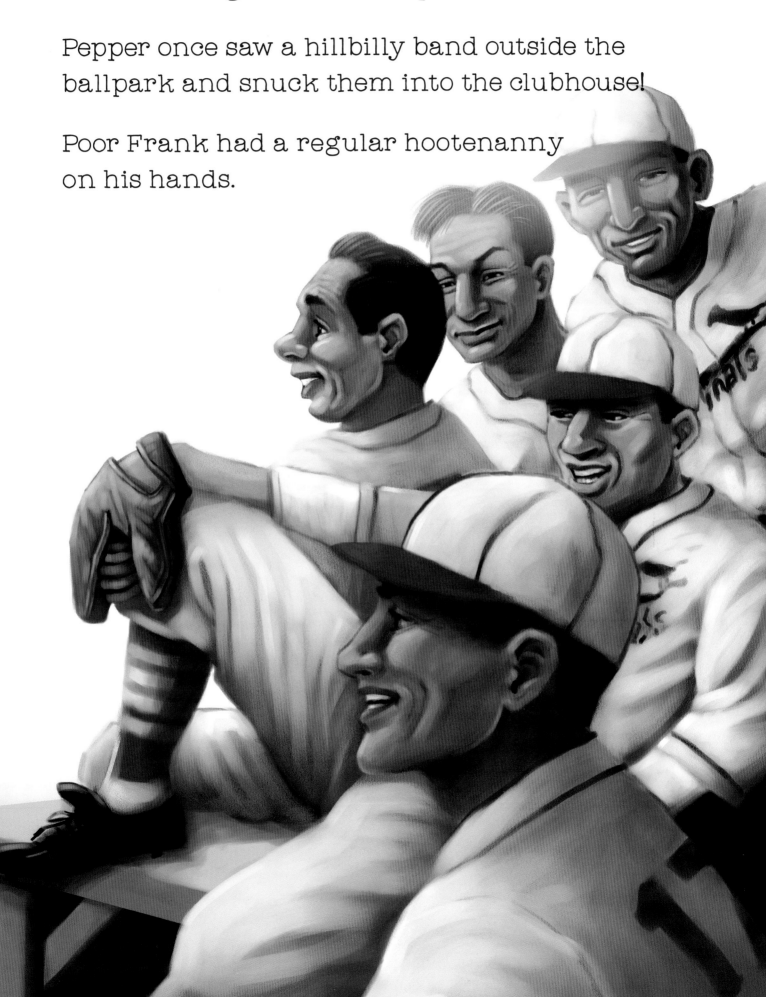

Sometimes, Dizzy's antics went too far.

Early in the 1934 season, he was bellyaching about how much the Cardinals paid him and his brother Paul, the team's second-best pitcher.

It got so bad the Dean brothers decided not to join the Cards for a road trip. Instead, they parked their cabooses under a tree and ate fried chicken as the team's train chugged by.

Frankie Frisch was mad, but Dizzy wasn't ready to apologize. In fact, HE TORE UP HIS UNIFORM!

CENTRAL

This just wouldn't do.

"Diz," Frank said, "you gotta be a leader for the Cardinals. You're the greatest pitcher in the league but you need to be a first-rate teammate too."

Frankie believed there was nothing Dizzy Dean couldn't do.

Like when he promised a hospital full of sick kids he'd strike out Giants batter Bill Terry with the bases loaded.

HE DID IT!

Or when he swore he and Paul would win at least 45 games in a season.

HE DID THAT TOO!

He rubbed elbows with fans.

He rallied his teammates.

And he **BAMBOOZLED** hitters.

Dizzy hurled the Gashouse
Gang right into the '34 Series
against the Tigers!

But he did more than pitch.

In Game 4 Dizzy volunteered to pinch run.
He was hightailing it to first when the pitcher
turned to throw for a double play.

WHACK

The ball hit him square in the head!

Up in the press box, I was relieved that Diz was okay.

When I asked him how he was feeling he said,
"The doc X-rayed my head. He found nothin'."

On October 9, 1934, Diz took the mound
for the deciding game.

He zipped pitch after pitch past hitters.

In the sixth inning, fans got mad at Cards
outfielder Joe Medwick for a hard slide and
started throwing all kinds of rubbish onto
the field!

"It's like they got themselves a grocery
store right under their seats!"
Dizzy shouted to Pepper.

Once the fans cooled down, Diz
was ready to bring home the win.

With two strikes in the ninth, he
wound up and delivered a fastball.

As the pitch whizzed toward the
plate, Dizzy turned to face his team.

He didn't have to watch the ball.

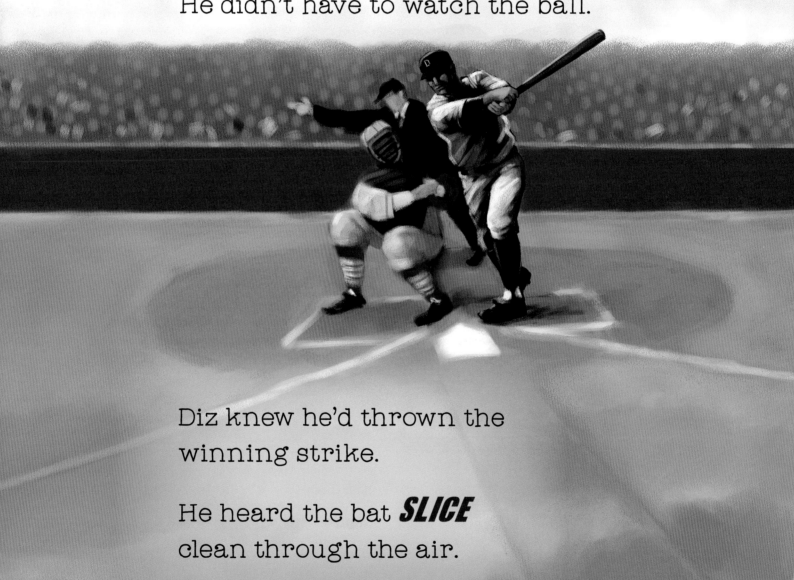

Diz knew he'd thrown the
winning strike.

He heard the bat **SLICE**
clean through the air.

THE CARDINALS WON THE WORLD SERIES!!!

With Dizzy Dean leading the way, the 1934 St. Louis Cardinals were World Champions!

Dizzy once told me it ain't braggin' if you can back it up.

I guess you can say he never did much braggin'.

Because our Dizzy could always back it up.